God Opens All Doors *in* Love *and* Devotion

God Opens All Doors *in* Love *and* Devotion

ROBERT E. MILLER

Paperback ISBN: 979-8-8229-1495-7
eBook ISBN: 979-8-8229-1496-4

Preface

This book represents my worship of God and His benevolent Son, Jesus Christ. As a devout Christian who believes in God and Jesus, I've matured spiritually over the years. As a poet, I hope you enjoy these spiritual poems and will share them with your family, friends, or fellow church members.

While growing up, something unexpected happened to me. No, I didn't become homeless, jump off a moving train, or lose a family member. But I did have a near-drowning experience. As an adult, I still occasionally think about what happened that day.

Over the years, I have listened to people on television talk shows discuss their death experiences of seeing lights or figures. Well, I don't remember having an experience such as those mentioned. Yet still, I feel the incident changed my life somehow. Spiritually, I don't know what to think since God renews the lives of people every day. Today, I can only say thank you, God, for showing your grace and letting me live another day of servitude to you on this beautiful earth.

Gratitude

Thank you for purchasing this book, and taking the time to rate it.

Heavenly Prayer

O Heavenly Father who turns darkness,
bringing forth light to everything we believe.
Bless us, O Lord, and give us the strength
to fight temptation every day. Amen.

Table of Contents

Genesis 1

Splendid Creator 2

Integrated Beliefs 3

Addictive Love 4

A Loving Father 5

The Power of Jesus 6

Beauty in You 7

Sweet Calvary 8

Restoration 9

Unselfishly Given 10

Mount Sinai 12

Prevailing Faith 13

Amazing God 14

Righteous Love 15

Rooted Faith 16

Blessings in Disguise 17

God's Love 18

Redeeming Souls 19

Unholy Thoughts 20

Turn to God 21

Faithful Spirits 22

Together Forever 23

Just Look Up 24

Paradise Shines 25

Unrighteous 26

Spiritual Delight 27

Merciful One 28

Convictions 29

Holy Light 30

Love Thee! 31

Wondrous Spirit 32

Anointed King 33

Fellowship 34

Benevolent Gifts 35

Self-Love 36

Ripe Fruits 37

Angels Dance 38

Anointed Grace 39

The Lord's Battle 40

Spiritual Connection 41

I Rise 42

Faithful Friend 43

Omnipotent One 44

Revealing Yourself 45

Genuine God 46

Eternal Peace 47

Spirits 48

Breath Taken 49

Path Chosen 50

Kneeling Down 51

Other Books to Consider Published by the Author 52

About the Author 53

Genesis

God created this beautiful earth.

When nature was observed in its original state, where

volumes of water flowed into rivers and streams, and God gave

birth to countless species, which gave precedent to His

creative work according to the Bible Scriptures.

Where the path to God

isn't always shaped.

When those stray

into darkness,

they can't escape.

Yet God still loves

them, despite their

mistakes. He offers them his

guidance along the way, so they'll

come to know His grace beyond the grave.

Splendid Creator

Gracious maker of all things.
Cherish my love for the goodness it brings.
Shine Your light deep within my heart.
So it will shine brighter than the star that
guided Noah's ark.
Their lives the splendid Creator I desire.
Far beyond the evening rainbow in the sky.
Where every day I can imagine hearing
His voice.
A wandering spirit that seeks His support
Here stands a humble servant, knocking at
His door, and waiting for Him to answer
with open arms.

Integrated Beliefs

We know we aren't alone, despite our foolish beliefs.

You know you guide our lives with no conditions.

You've been the bridge to fulfilling our dreams.

For amazing phrases that we can't explain.

Where our hearts sing out in holy praise.

Knowing you're the God who directs our path.

A wonderful feeling for which we have no regrets.

Where we can find comfort with You and Your Son.

Who possesses our spirits to pray each morning.

A rewarding experience that opens our eyes.

To steadfast souls touched by Your love.

As the secret to our lives relies on faith.

Knowing that Your words live inside us.

Where we have trust in You to take away our fears.

Which gives us the strength to kneel before You.

Addictive Love

We're not worthy, Lord, for everything you've done.

Our hearts speak to You more and more.

Even when our lives seemed out of control.

The gravity of our faith kept growing.

Amid the many emotions that evoke our souls.

Now we find ourselves addicted to Your love.

This exuberant feeling, which we cannot describe,

has shaped our convictions like no other.

As Your love fills our hearts with so much joy.

It feels like a wave of emotions has taken over our minds.

Where we find ourselves now addicted to Your love.

As Your love grows stronger every day, we're alive.

A Loving Father

You're our light beyond heaven's gate

When You lifted our hearts to an anointed faith.

Then, You awakened our minds to the gifts we possess.

And gave us the Savior, who took away our sins.

You called us your beloved children.

But at first, we struggled to believe.

Afterward, we learned the truth in your words,

that we can't get out of our heads.

Then, You transformed our lives to show us you care.

And You took our hands, despite our reluctance to go.

Unsure of our feelings, which caught us off guard.

You showed us your finest grace to settle our hearts.

You're the beloved Father, to whom we confess our sins.

The One we call upon to change our lives.

An eternal figure whose passion warms our hearts

The Father of Creation to whom we give ourselves.

The Power of Jesus

Hail Him, the orchestrator of faith!
He who stands before his Father unwaveringly.
A beckoning servant as a mustard seed.
The dominant force that needs no redemption
He who preserved righteous words for us to believe,
To affirm His Father as the creator of humanity.
And so gives His everlasting union and love,
To prepare His children for the afterlife beyond.

Beauty in You

When I walk through holy water,
I know I'm not alone.
Your presence is my source of joy.
My lungs are filled with Your love.
No storms will keep us apart.
You've always guarded my heart.

When Your beauty blinds my eyes
My heart feels You even more.
When life stress weighs me down,
Your steadfast love kept me going.
Every time sin tempted my faith,
You came to my rescue every day.

When Your faith captured my heart.
Your words shape my every thought.
I know that I'm not alone,
Your undying faith keeps me going.
My life is no longer on edge.
I can feel my childhood laughter again.

When You took hold of my dreams.
I knew I was Your finest masterpiece.
Nothing will break us apart.
You're the bread that nourishes my heart.

Sweet Calvary

I pour out my tears for you.

I hope you'll hear my prayers.

As I wear the scars of life,

You can only heal.

My heart sings out in praise,

and binds my faith to You.

I celebrate the gifts of life

That no sinner can rebuke,

to know the sweet Calvary.

It's something familiar in my heart

Nothing that death can interrupt.

Your name stands above all

When You surround me with your love.

As You'll bless my soul in the heavens above.

Restoration

God wants to heal your broken heart.

And take away the misery hidden in the dark.

Amid the pain that surrounds your life.

He knows of the evil that lurks within.

Where it ignites hatred to control your mind.

Of unchristian beliefs to distort your joy.

That prevents you from hearing His voice,

And receive His mercy without any judgment.

Unselfishly Given

You give yourself unselfishly.
The God of the mountain
The God we come to love
You catch our hearts on fire and cleanse
our souls.
You give our lives purpose, showing us
that you care.

Through difficult times, we sought you out.
Knowing you'd renew our faith and not
judge our sins.
You gave us pardons we didn't deserve.
You anchored our hearts when they
trembled in fear.

You're the God of the mountain
The God of our souls
The owner of our faith whom we walk with.

We stand humble and stumble no more.
Where we reflect on everything you've done,
As we baptize ourselves to You.
We feel a sense of inner peace
that you can only give.
We cherish your presence.
That has taken hold of us.

You gave our lives purpose.
And You shield our hearts from relentless shame
Knowing you're the God of the mountain
That we've grown to love
The Father of our beliefs
Where our faith erupts, knowing
everything you've done.
As we give ourselves to you.
The Father above!

Mount Sinai

Show me, O Lord, thy divine life.
Amid the clouds of Mount Sinai
Lay thy soundness of holy praise.
Of prayers only meant for angels' ears
Which harnesses tunes to cross lilies and dunes
That echoes the sounds of God's holy power
Helping those faithless find their way
So they'll shed the darkness for the light of faith

Prevailing Faith

Thou taketh on the beliefs of the world.
Knowing thy heart can't endure.
Where it was overcome by the abundance of sin.
When it had yielded to the devil's whim.
Wherefore, God cast his light into the darkness.
Knowing His righteousness would prevail,
even in the purgatory of hell.
The sovereignty of God shall never disappear.
It embodies the source of life.
To those who gracefully accept His gifts,
and faithfully come to Him.

Amazing God

Just imagine the afterlife to come.

While the vast universe surrounds your soul.

Where God's angels sing along with "Amazing Grace."

As Jesus teaches in the school of belief.

There, He quotes lines from a verse of Psalms.

And souls practice the scriptures by reciting poems.

As they memorize each meaning of God's word.

That heaven is alive with omnipotent power.

Not just a story studied by biblical scholars.

Quote: Amazing Grace by John Newton

Righteous Love

God knew you in your mother's womb
Thus granted you favor on a full moon.
The God who whispers love in your ear.
With old-fashioned love, you didn't choose
The God that wants to transform your heart.
And thus gives the gospel to you for support.
Of unbreakable words to sharpen your thoughts.
From a merciful God who loves you a lot
Who gives you the wisdom to test your faith?
With compassionate love to temper your heart
So that He may transcend you to love yourself,
And instill His inspiration to give you hope.
For an unrestrained love that never lets go.

Rooted Faith

Jesus, you were God's promise of eternal life.

Your name shall forever be inscribed in our hearts.

You made the faithless rethink their lives.

Whenever Your name was spoken out loud.

It scared the Pharisees, Romans, and crowds.

You, the beloved Jesus who died to be reborn,

We sing to You.

We pray to You.

Knowing our faith is the key to our lives,

and the love You give is rooted in our hearts.

We look to You.

We worship You.

We give ourselves to You.

Blessings in Disguise

Lord of the Holy Spirit,
We can't get you off our minds.
We're not sure if we'll survive.
You've been our source of hope,
and the voice beyond the cross.

You're the truth that sinners can't forsake.
The Immortal, whom we worship for support.
Where we would like to feel Your heart in ours.
So we may experience the serenity of Your joy

You said you would love us forever
As we come to depend on you.
You've been our source of motivation.
The obvious reason for our lives
We can't get you off our minds.

Whenever we were in doubt,
You were the One to clear our thoughts
When problems occupy our lives.
You've been the light to brighten things up.
We can't get You off our minds
Because You're the God of the Kingdom above.

God's Love

God will love you today and tomorrow.

He knows the struggles of life.

The uphill battles you might face,

even your pain and suffering,

God loves all things.

He loves the blades of grass,

the vastness of the seas, and

the birds that sing in harmony.

God's love is unique.

His love conquers even envy and hate,

and brings peace to all things.

He can turn every day's unhappiness into joy,

despair into belief,

life's agonies into pleasantries.

Redeeming Souls

Give Him praise as you lay palms
at His feet, and a godly man that
comes to redeem our sins.
Forsaken onto Him, the threat
of death, knowing His betrayal
was already in progress.
A faithful Son, who honored His
Father, by teaching the truth in His
word to sinners and nonbelievers.
So they'll come to believe in Him
and know that salvation is real.
To know Him is to know His Father, and
ask for His forgiveness and redemption.

Unholy Thoughts

Lord, unholy voices keep swirling in our minds.

Each one tries to destroy everything we've done.

As they solicit emotions we can't describe.

Of ungodly feelings that were odd to our minds.

Where they keep us asking questions about our design.

As we call upon you, Lord, to calm these thoughts,

and provide us with the strength we need to survive.

Amid the uncharted waters of a destiny sought.

Here stand devoted servants to you, Lord, who

want to live a life of blessings and servitude.

Turn to God

Whenever you can't breathe.
When you're under a lot of stress
Turn to God; He'll be there.
He'll come to your rescue every time.
Whatever the outcome.
He'll be your crusader to part the waves
and take you through waters never surveyed.
Turn to God, and He'll guide you along the way.
Whenever life becomes unbearable to live.
God knows of the hardships as Jesus did
He promised that He would grant you eternal life.
Where He wants to become your source of relief.
And restore the happiness that had resigned in you.
Where He'll always be with you every step of the way,
And make your life manageable even in the darkest days.

Faithful Spirits

Nature bathes in the presence of God's light,

Where it reignites His flames of creation.

And tirelessly gives us His divine gifts,

That guides us to come to Him,

and with the abundance of each belief.

Within the brilliance of His holiness,

He knows our lives belong to Him.

Despite the evil that resides within, and

He wants to renew our unholy hearts,

To a time of peace and harmony.

Where we'll forever find grace in His love

As it was in the beginning!

Together Forever

Let Jesus wipe away your tears and
energize your thoughts.
He knows he'll be the glory now and
forever in your life
"Belief in me," said Jesus, "I am in the Father
and the Father is in me."
So my Father may lift your burdens and
restore your beliefs.
And heal your broken hearts and reshape
your mind.
Where He shall preserve your soul for
eternity.

ESV Bible quote: John 14:11

Just Look Up

Where have you gone?
When our lives are falling apart.
You've always been our support.
When others try to divide our hearts.
You were the One who fought for us.
When the Savior comes, we'll find some relief.
You know you're the righteous one we need.
Where have you gone?
When sin has taken hold of our hearts.
You've always been the bridge we must cross.
Whenever we stumble in our beliefs,
You were the redeemer we needed.
When the world appears so dark.
Your presence is needed to bring things back.
Where have you gone?
When children don't have enough to eat,
As evil tries to lay waste to creation.
And heaven is only a short distance away.
You alone, you alone, we can only trust
when we look up and try to figure things out.
As we need Your help to calm our thoughts.

Paradise Shines

The stars of heaven twinkle for you and
me.
They're the lights God shines in our eyes.
So He may brighten up our lives, and
we bear witness to His amazing gifts.
He who wakes us up daily before we can
pray.
Then He casts out our sins to increase our
faith.
This was God's way of transforming our
lives across planes of reality, we can't
visualize.
Which shapes the ministry to entice
our minds.
Through the biblical scriptures written on
Mount Sinai
There God enlightened the spirits, we
possess, and gave his mercy to those with
unholy beliefs.
So they come to know of His forgiveness
and embrace the truth of His word.

Unrighteous

Oh, silent ones, praise the Lord

Where the unrighteous speak lies against God.

They lash out in dissatisfaction.

Yet God offers them love, but evil owns their tongues.

As they reject the blessings of God's gifts,

and His righteousness.

But joy still comes in the morning, and

God's love of forgiveness validates all hearts.

That gives hope to the weary who need His support.

Spiritual Delight

Tranquility amid a roaring storm

That brings forth trust in the Lord,

For Him to heal the discontent and wretchedly weak.

Given to Christians, the truthfulness of belief

To overcome life's unsatisfying days.

On triumphant opportunities to embrace,

To stand beside the Lord Almighty Himself,

And receive His wisdom and edifying words.

Where He'll fulfill your Christian desire,

To know Him spiritually in His time.

Merciful One

The sun rises amid God's trees, as it

brings forth an array of colorful days.

Where spiritual lights flow into beautiful streams.

While God's angels listen to his angelic phrases.

As they faithfully serve Him every day.

And give Him thanks for his unselfish ways.

Convictions

You baptized us, Lord, in Christian beliefs.

Where our convictions now run deep,

And our lives have found new meaning.

It's a wondrous experience that we come to enjoy.

Knowing we can entrust everything to Your will.

Even when sin came knocking at our door.

It was a defining moment that stimulated our minds.

We ignored all rational behavior, which we can't explain.

It was an unbelievable feeling that caused us to pray.

As we repent our sins before You this day.

Knowing your forgiveness is all we need.

For a merciful God who gives himself freely.

Who brought light to the darkness that had risen in us.

And then You renew our convictions with no mistrust.

Holy Light

What if my life was a mistake?

The path I walked was another.

Everything I knew was on a different plane,

and ideas about life were like shadows in a maze

Amid the enigmatic figures that reflect the light,

which I couldn't distinguish because of their brightness.

That possessed a great source of incredible power,

which was devoted to God's covenant and glory.

Love Thee!

How does God love thee?

Thou shall know the many ways

He loves thee through pain and rage.

He loves thee with every breath taken.

Beyond the mercy given to thee.

He loves thee in a rebellious state.

He loves thee through life's burdens and mistakes.

He loves thee with the utmost respect

Amid the celebration of life and death.

He loves thee with no regrets.

Wondrous Spirit

O, Holy Father of the living light
You're the source of our faithful hearts
Among every soul shining in Your light.
You transcend those with spiritual insight.
As You give hope to sinners seeking relief.
You're the good shepherd who gathers His sheep.
An ever-present spirit that transforms what we think.
The Father, whose knowledge is within our reach.
The immortal figure who knows everything we do.

Anointed King

O Lord, the Father of the angels above

Entrust your love to our broken souls.

So Jesus may walk among us as before.

Just like the old days in Jerusalem

Where believers came to embrace God's work.

Knowing that Jesus was the Messiah

The anointed King who came to strengthen our faith.

To transform the lives of those unbelieving minds.

So they find favor in God's love and

the rewards of His eternal blessings.

Fellowship

One must go into the valley of despair,

onto the scales of God with the purest heart.

So that you may seek fellowship with Christ

and be reborn according to the gospel.

Blessed be the Father for His eternal grace.

For Jesus, who lifted the weight off

our shoulders in Jerusalem.

And He silenced those liars who

conspired against Him and freed His

flesh from persecution.

Whence brought forth His resurrection,

and sanctification of God's affection.

Benevolent Gifts

God gives us His mercy and
the immense beauty that surrounds us.
As the sun rises, and the moon
pushes against the ocean tides,
and with the abundance of
good deeds you perform, they won't
be enough to get you into heaven.
"Commit your work to the Lord,
and your plans will be established."
And in His righteousness,
you shall receive immeasurable
gifts that you can treasure.

ESV Bible quote: Proverb 16:3.

Self-Love

You stared into God's mirror.

That was a reflection of yourself.

But only seen through the eyes of God.

It was an earthly experience that stuck in your mind.

To know God loves you no matter what

It reinforced the faith you had inside.

As it awakened great memories,

no longer drifting against the tide.

At a time when you'll live a life of

righteousness to never die.

Ripe Fruits

The spirit of God's gospel bears hidden seeds.

Seeds that laid the foundation for humanity.

Through the awakening of spiritual hope.

Untarnished by wickedness staining our blood,

Of the senseless cruelty the devil brought forth.

Who is unable to transcend the love of God?

Or cross the planes of our inner hearts

In the adventurous seeds of faith and glory,

There lies a covenant of unbroken beliefs.

Whence bear the ripe fruits of His righteousness.

The God of the mountains and the valleys beneath

His mercy comes in the sweetness of His fruit.

That transforms the reality that we perceive.

Given us the gospel of His hospitality,

And the seeds of greatness on which bear His name.

That lay the foundation that we shall live,

with the God of heaven and the fertile earth.

Angels Dance

Two of God's angels tiptoed down on earth.

They twisted and turned like spinning tops on glass.

Their bodies moved in ways no human could describe.

Angels dancing like Ginger Rogers and Fred Astaire.

One dance they performed was awesome to see.

Open wings without shoes while doing the moonwalk on-air.

A wonderful performance that God's angels gave.

They deserved a standing ovation for dancing that day.

Anointed Grace

Our Father, the perfect Shepherd of Grace
The Creator, whose wisdom we come to embrace.
The truth about everything we hold so dear.
The Father, whose word keeps our hearts sincere.
Yet an immortal spirit, in which we live to serve.
The Lord of Lords, who protects all souls.
Where He became the antidote for our sins.
For an infection, we had taken in.
As He awakens us to a spiritual cure.
Through a child that was born in Bethlehem.
Mercifully, He planted faith in our shallow minds.
And His anointed blessings He spread over time.

The Lord's Battle

No matter what you're going through.
My dear brothers and sisters, stand firm.
The Lord shall always be there to safeguard you,
And fight the battles you might face.
He's aware of your stressors and mistakes.
Through high tides and loss of faith,
God shall bless you no matter the place.
And stand behind you if you stray,
regardless of your religion, belief, or faith.
The Lord shall be Your anchor for eternity

Spiritual Connection

My God is the protector of my soul.

The anointed Father of the life I know.

He's the administrator of faith against pagan beliefs.

A charismatic gift who gives Himself willingly.

Whereupon my lips become clay to His words.

While He shapes my spirit, for this I am grateful.

So that someday I will come to receive eternal life.

Thus, accept Him forever with a loving heart.

And spiritually bathe in His holy water.

Then be worthy of receiving His heavenly rewards.

I Rise

O Lord, you're the light that creates my dreams.

The tears I wipe when you whisper in my ears.

You're the morning sunlight that nourishes my soul.

My favorite friend who'll never let me go.

You're the protector I depend on to fulfill my beliefs.

The eternal spirit I kneel before to strengthen my knees.

I rise, no longer wondering who you are.

I rise with Your convictions in my heart.

I rise to Your light that shines over mountaintops.

I rise for a God who knows my broken thoughts.

I rise to a God who directs my path.

I rise to a God who keeps my faith intact.

I rise

I rise

I rise.

Faithful Friend

I'll praise you, Father,
when I kneel at your throne,
and rejoice in your presence.
Knowing You're the God I love.

You, who sat beside me,
when I needed a friend.
You settled my heart,
whenever it was in pain.
You are not just the Lord God,
nor a prayer, which I recite at night.
But the alpha and omega of life,
and the creator of everything.

You're the Goodfather,
who'll raise us from the grave.
The redeemer I'll die to know,
And the eternal spirit of my soul.
You who grants salvation,
whoever believes in you.
And accepts the gospel of
Your word only
sanctified by You.

Omnipotent One

We win battles on our knees.

Every time, we give praise to God Almighty.

He's the inner power within our souls.

The God we live for and yearn to behold.

An Omnipotent One, whom we can turn to for support.

When we travel down paths, we can't escape.

Our faith becomes the compass that determines our fate.

Amongst the many obstacles and trials, we must face,

God gives us the chance to change our lives,

And the Holy Bible to transform our minds.

Revealing Yourself

God designed you for greatness,

with the beauty of heaven inside.

It's a testament to His love,

which the devil despises.

He who gave you spiritual food,

so you'd know His word

And submit yourself to Him,

so you can know the truth.

As it flourished in the heart of Jesus.

He who washed away your sins.

To reveal the perfect soul within,

so that you'll have everlasting peace,

and a new beginning.

Genuine God

Our faith lives deep in our hearts.

It's where God dwells.

He's the body and soul we possess,

And not a false God of what atheists think.

But an astute leader to whom we give our praise.

Yet a revered figure whose love is precise,

And He needs no permit to enter our lives.

Where He wears no mask to hide behind.

He's the Father whose love requires no test.

An omnipotent God deserves our respect.

He hears our prayers, even when we're sick.

It's something He does out of reflex.

Eternal Peace

My soul rises upwardly, beyond the
shores of earthly men
Where it crosses the plains of
my inner dreams and into the endless
beauty of heaven.
There resides the splendid Creator I
desire.
A soul that beckons to be far, far
away from a deceitful world, where
I shall rest in peace.

Spirits

Invisibility has
no apparent shape
Even ghosts, who aren't
drawn to themselves
Obscured images
of reflective light
They're only visible
when the moon is bright.
Unfamiliar apparitions
that play tricks on the eyes.
Ghostly figures that aren't alive
Benevolent souls trapped in time
That gives the illusion of hell itself.

Breath Taken

Every time we wish upon a star
God reaches down to touch our hearts.
He whose breath rests in our lungs
And designed the universe before our eyes.

He who knows the truth in our hearts
Where faith becomes a matter of belief.
And judgment is for Him to deliver.
The God who celebrates the love we give
And accepts all our earthly fears.

Thus, He rejoices when we turn to Him.
The God who harvests our every thought,
And wants to transform our hearts.
When we give thanks to Him for His love,
And all the wonderful things He has done.

Path Chosen

You chose the path of life to walk,

with God's guidance, never thought.

You're not a lost soul drifting at sea.

But a devoted servant to God Almighty

Yet you are filled with incredible beliefs.

Knowing God's voice lives inside of you

That disclaims any closet faith you had.

For heavenly words, you couldn't analyze.

To the external forces, you try to define.

That amazes you every minute and hour.

In a God-given body that controls your life.

Kneeling Down

We come to you, Lord.

We're kneeling on our knees.

Can you see us?

We don't have a cause to enjoy; we've given it all,

but the rain still comes.

It took away our sunshine, despite everything we've done.

You've been our refuge; we turn to you when our strength is gone.

We listen to Your words, which have taken hold of us.

We come to You.

Knowing our fight isn't over till we can shake off our grief,

And receive the power of Your blessings to set us free.

You lifted our spirits, so we could see.

And to know You fight our battles with no conditions.

We come to You.

You've been our inspiration whenever we

needed a friend.

You gave our lives purpose, which we could only feel.

Then, You inspired us to pray daily,

to change our ways.

We come to You.

You have been our firm foundation.

Our steadfast source of strength.

The eternal Father, we live to worship,

and the giver of every blessing.

Other Books to Consider
Published by the Author

April's Rain Must Fall (2022), Palmetto Publishing

No Longer Spiritually Blind (2020), Xulon Publishing

The Madness Behind Poetry (2019), Newman Springs Publishing

About the Author

Robert is an American author living in Louisville, Kentucky. Robert received his bachelor's degree at the University of Cincinnati. He's a devoted Christian, believes in God, and studies the teachings of Jesus. Robert attends church services every week and enjoys reading Christian texts, Bible scripture, and daily devotions.

Robert E. Miller

Bearcat412001@Yahoo.com

www.ingramcontent.com/pod-product-compliance
Lightning Source LLC
Chambersburg PA
CBHW060910130726
48001CB00006B/2182